After the Move

Judith Lechman

A LION BOOK
Oxford · Batavia · Sydney

Text copyright © 1990 Judith Lechman
This edition copyright © 1990 Lion Publishing

All rights reserved

Published by
Lion Publishing Corporation
1705 Hubbard Avenue, Batavia, Illinois 60510, USA
ISBN 0 7459 1813 1

First edition 1990

Library of Congress Cataloging-in-Publication Data

Lechman, Judith C.
  After the move / Judith Lechman. — 1st ed.
    p. cm.
  ISBN 0-7459-1813-1
  I. Moving, Household — Psychological aspects.   I. Title.
TX307.L43   1990
155.9'4 — dc20

Printed and bound in Great Britain by
Cox & Wyman Ltd, Reading

Contents

1	Transplant Shock	5
2	Letting Go of Fear	7
3	Beware the Nostalgia Trap	10
4	A Family Affair	13
5	Marriage and Moving	16
6	Relocation and the Single Person	19
7	Being Disoriented	22
8	Being Disorganized	25
9	Being Discouraged	29
10	Being Disconnected	32
11	Befriending	36
12	Reconnecting	39
13	Moving Forward	42
14	Flourishing Anew	44

Moving is among life's most stressful events.

1

Transplant Shock

Arms filled with groceries, I hurried across the crowded parking lot. Halfway to my car, I stopped and looked around in dismay. No familiar faces. No friendly words.

People rushed by, tight-lipped and unsmiling. Even the flat horizon seemed silent and cold. Nothing about my new town felt warm or welcoming.

Tears filled my eyes as I remembered my former home in the mountains, two thousand miles away. It hurt to recall the friends I left behind. Yet it hurt more to deny how deeply I missed them.

I had no one but myself to blame. When our family agreed to move across the country, I closed down emotionally. I foolishly refused to admit my grief over leaving a community I loved, hoping to avoid the loss I was sure to feel.

My feelings were only natural. Moving is among life's most stressful events. Only death and divorce bring a greater sense of separation and loss. And whether we choose to move or are forced to move, this upheaval in our lives can cause real and deep pain.

Moving shatters the reassuring comfort of our daily routines. Even worse, it severs almost all ties with our old communities — ties that took years to develop. In our new homes, nothing yet fills this void.

Uprooted and disconnected, we wonder if we will ever become successful transplants. Lonely and afraid, we long for the safety of familiar places and faces. Missing the cheerful environment in our old office or that close friend down the street, we question why we ever agreed to move.

These feelings are as much a part of moving as packing boxes or setting up utilities. We should expect them. Every move brings its own case of Transplant Shock.

To survive Transplant Shock, we simply need to admit our loneliness, our doubts, and our fears. Accepting these normal feelings is the first step in growing happy and healthy roots after the move.

2

Letting Go of Fear

Moving makes the bravest among us feel lost and afraid. All at once we find ourselves working for a new company, living in a strange new home, and finding our way around a confusing new neighborhood.

At work, we realize that our new coworkers don't know anything about us. Will they recognize our talents? Will they share our likes and dislikes? How well will we work together?

At home, we wonder if the strangers next door will welcome or resent us. Will we become good neighbors or real friends?

Moving means proving ourselves to others all over again. Since we share no common history, we have no choice but to start on the ground floor in developing personal and work-related relationships.

Starting anew brings us face to face with our earliest fears.

A self-assured friend once confided that whenever she's about to be transferred, she feels much the

Will our new coworkers recognize our talents?

same as when she left the security of home for nursery school.

Her stomach tightens. A lump rises in her throat. Tears threaten to spill. The past suddenly looks golden, while the future becomes a dark pit filled with every imaginable childhood fear of loss and abandonment.

"How do you hide it so well?" I asked her.

"I don't hide it. I've learned to let go of it," she explained. "Whenever I'm in the midst of a move, I use a little exercise I created.

"As I wash my face each morning, I remind myself that I'm no longer a child. Then I list all the fears I can dream up. Silly or serious, big or small, I say each fear aloud. Finally, while rinsing my face, I let go of them one at a time.

"I wash them all away."

After my last move, I followed my friend's advice and noticed a strange thing happening. My list of fears grew shorter. By the end of the third week, they sounded more like complaints than legitimate fears.

To me, this exercise is more than a child's game of make-believe. It brings my fears out into the open. As a Christian I believe that God is greater than all of them. He is in charge of this world. He loves me and wants what is best for me.

Stating my fears aloud robs them of their awesome power to paralyze me. Knowing that God will help me face any situation, however difficult, I can meet new challenges with growing confidence.

Moving doesn't have to be an invitation to fear. Instead, it can be an open door to new opportunities, ideas, people, and places.

3
Beware the Nostalgia Trap

Nostalgia is big business. Airwaves hum with songs and images of decades past, linking our fondest memories to advertisers' products.

Each time I hear a favorite song used as background music in an advertisement, I remember Maria, a wise and witty woman who lived in a nursing home where I once worked. She had led a richly varied life but strongly disliked reminiscing about her past.

"Looking backwards is a trap! Nostalgia is a sentimental liar!" she would exclaim.

More often than not, we fall directly into the nostalgia trap. As the old song goes, we tend to accentuate the positive and eliminate the negative when we sort through memories of life before the move.

The present pales in comparison with "the good old days." Seen through an idealized lens, our former neighbors are kinder, our coworkers more helpful, and our communities trouble-free.

We ignore the nights when our neighbor's dog kept us awake with its incessant barking.

We conveniently forget the monthly free-for-alls at the school-board meetings. We ignore the nights when our neighbor's German shepherd kept us awake with its incessant barking. We overlook the aggravation caused by gossiping coworkers.

With each new telling, our former homes grow grander and our hometowns more attractive. In reality, the house needed a new roof and the town required a face-lift. We forget the times of worry and self-doubt, anger and disgust, heartache and sorrow.

Our move will go smoother if we are realistic about the past. Seeing the past through rose-colored glasses does a real disservice to the people we have known and those who will become a part of our lives.

Maria realized that sentimental lies send out weak roots that cannot support our old relationships or nurture the new. Yes, we need to cherish the past. But only by being honest about the past can we move smoothly into the future.

Ted, a relative who moves his family frequently, knows the importance of sidestepping the nostalgia trap. He sees each transfer to a new community as an opportunity to put the past into perspective.

Ted, his wife, and their two sons enjoy remembering funny stories and sad moments shared in their last home. As a family, they clear the air of unrealistic memories and excitedly look to the future.

By honestly remembering the past and confidently anticipating the future, they embrace the present — the place where new roots begin.

4
A Family Affair

Adults seldom move by themselves. According to statistics from five international moving companies, families with children account for the majority of corporate-sponsored moves.

Parents realize how difficult a move can be for their youngsters. We hear their grousing and complaining, feel their pain in leaving friends behind, commiserate with their loneliness, and suffer their awkward entry into a confusing new world.

Like adults, children have varying reactions to the stress of moving. Some withdraw. Others throw themselves into frantic activity. Some hide their feelings. Others talk nonstop.

Whether it's with silence or tears, energy or sulking, our children go through tough times in moving.

Our children need to know that we empathize. Nothing helps dispel fear and sadness so much as sharing our feelings with those we love most. Even

Some children throw themselves into frantic activity.

though "More people, more problems" might be an accurate appraisal of the challenges of a family move, I prefer to say, "The more, the merrier!"

Yet keeping the lines of communication open during the hustle and bustle of moving isn't as simple as it sounds. Hearing what our children are really telling us comes only through patient practice.

A child's whining or grumbling may mean something quite different from a temporary case of ill-humor. It could be masking frustration, uncertainty, anger, or a host of other emotions unexpressed as yet.

We have to learn to listen to our family members with an inner ear tuned to their pain and joy. We can't get so wrapped up in the busyness of moving that we forget to share ourselves with our children.

There's a wonderful Chinese saying: Talking doesn't cook the rice. It reminds me that sharing feelings, in itself, won't keep the lines of family communication wide open. Talking is essential, but doing activities together is just as important. And at no time is it more important than while moving.

These activities can be helpful during the early days of moving in:

☐ Leave the curtain-hanging and take a walk with your child. Map out the route to the new school or bus stop.

☐ Stop unpacking long enough to discover the local park. Try out the slides and swings with your preschooler.

☐ Rather than put up pictures, find the community tennis courts and play several sets with your teenager. Both the exercise and the communication will do your heart good.

Talking opens the gates to creating a positive family move, but doing things together carries us successfully through them.

5

Marriage and Moving

A generation ago, husbands switched jobs and moved across the country while their wives trailed along, making homes comfortable and settling children in school.

Today, eleven percent of trailing spouses are men. Women who move because of their husband's new job often must find their own job as well. Due to the economic climate, the trailing spouse can rarely afford to put a career on hold. While one spouse begins adjusting to a new job, then, the other faces the stress of job-hunting.

My new neighbors, Priscilla and Greg, are one such couple. Together, they spent the past Sunday making a list dividing moving-related duties between them. With both of them beginning new jobs, they wondered how they would ever handle all the chores.

As they made their way down the list — deciding who would call the moving company, arrange garbage service, find a family doctor, and register their automobiles — they both came to the same wishful

Eleven percent of trailing spouses are men.

conclusion: "We need a wife!"

For many couples, coping with change is a full-time job. More and more husbands and wives are discovering that moving affects their relationship on every level from the financial to the emotional.

Short tempers and fast-food meals are temporary annoyances. Other problems will take more time and understanding to resolve. Some spouses half-heartedly leave rising careers, family, friends, or educational opportunities to be with their partners. Their anger, resentment, and frustration are then unpacked along with the household goods — often to the amazement of the "offending" spouse.

In the past decade, specialized firms have sprung up to help marriage partners work through these new and often conflicting concerns.

☐ Human-resources consultants assist with job-search seminars, give networking aid and run employment placement bureaus.

☐ Private relocation services offer everything from house-hunting assistance to personal shopping guides for the working couple.

☐ Real-estate companies routinely give information on family neighborhood services, while corporations have added support groups for the spouses of relocated employees.

☐ Community organizations offer monthly programs for newcomers to meet one another and learn more about the history and cultural opportunities in the area.

☐ Churches invite new people to attend worship services, coffee hours, and social activities. In addition, many churches offer practical help and professional counseling, often at little or no charge. Those who already belong to a church have a head start: They are already part of a ready-made community.

Most communities offer at least a few of these relocation programs. Find out what is available in yours. This kind of help can make the task of putting down new roots infinitely easier.

6

Relocation and the Single Person

When single people move, they leave behind more than a network of professional contacts. Often they are moving away from family and friends. They no longer have anyone nearby who can help them in a crisis, lend a sympathetic shoulder, lift their spirits, or share a laugh.

In a high-school faculty dining room the other day, I made an informal survey of how the single teachers present felt about moving.

"Arranging to have the utilities turned on just about unhinged me."

"With housing so expensive, I couldn't afford anything but an apartment. Unfortunately, most places don't allow pets."

"I've never gotten used to coming home to an empty house."

"In the short run, my greatest problem was setting up bank and utility accounts. In the long run, loneliness."

What surprised me most about the answers was

their almost complete agreement. It didn't matter what age or sex the teachers were, or if they were

---

A Do and Don't List for the Single Person

☐ Do leave work behind and socialize. Don't marry your job to fill the empty hours.

☐ Do become involved in a company-sponsored activity, such as a bowling league or music group. Don't isolate yourself at work.

☐ Do be visible and become part of a special-interest group. Do join a health club, a computer club, a Bible study group, or an adult-education class. Don't spend your leisure time cocooning at home.

☐ Do recognize that married couples and families face equally difficult challenges in moving. Don't wallow in self-pity, thinking that no one else feels overwhelmed in the midst of moving.

recently single, always single, widowed or divorced. The complaints and problems were the same.

☐ Do find others with whom you can begin to share your new experiences, confusion, obstacles, and dreams. Don't fall into the trap of self-imposed loneliness.

☐ Above all else, do understand that other people feel the same fear, hesitancy, and doubts that you are experiencing right now. Don't be timid about asking for help.

7

Being Disoriented

In the days following the move, we will undoubtedly experience each of the Four Ds. At some time or another, we will feel Disoriented, Disorganized, Discouraged, and Disconnected.

Being disoriented is perhaps the smallest yet most annoying obstacle blocking our paths to a successful move. Simply put, when we arrive in a new community, we don't know where we are or how we will get to where we need to go.

We spend countless hours getting lost in search of the most basic services. We can't find our way to the grocery store and, once there, we don't know where to find our favorite foods. Having been referred to a doctor and dentist, we have to hunt for their offices. Going out to a movie requires hours of planning.

Getting lost threatens to become a permanent way of life.

Getting lost threatens to become a permanent way of life.

Thankfully, being disoriented in our new hometown is a temporary experience. We will learn our way around. Streets will become familiar. Landmarks will reassure us that we are heading in the right direction — at least some of the time.

Frequent movers have a number of ways to deal with disorientation. Some newcomers buy detailed street and county maps to chart exactly where they are going and the best way to get there.

Some, expecting to get lost, build time into their schedules for stopping to ask directions as they travel.

Others take an analytical approach, writing down unusual places and street names. One friend learned his routes to work and shopping by memorizing the restaurants he passed every day.

The method for battling disorientation is less important than our overall attitude. Whether we approach it haphazardly or methodically, we will appreciate the process more if we see it as an opportunity to discover everything our new hometown has to offer.

Every area has a distinctive personality reflecting the people who live and work there. Enjoy the hours of exploration. If we think positively, winding our way to the auto mechanic or poking around the neighborhood deli holds the promise of adventure.

8

Being Disorganized

When we move into a new house or start work in a new office, we usually find that we can't find anything at all. From can openers to copier paper, nothing seems to be where we need or expect it. Minor tasks take on major proportions.

Moving can make the most organized person feel hopelessly muddled. A veteran of many moves, I've developed a simple system for battling the disorganized-household blues.

Following the dictum that cleanliness is next to godliness, I make certain that my new house is clean before I unpack the first box. Then I attack the household goods in the order of basic survival needs.

The kitchen is my top priority. The bedrooms and baths follow in order.

Only when I've taken care of food, sleep, grooming, and work areas do I consider unpacking the

Organizing the kitchen is my top priority. ▶

dining room, living room, or den. And once I've begun a room, I stay there until it's finished.

This system works only if you keep two critical rules: Stop being a perfectionist and start practicing stick-to-itiveness.

The first rule means being willing to lower your expectations of yourself and others. On several occasions I've reminded myself that it was all right to misplace the silverware tray, the one kitchen item I manage to lose during every move.

I've also learned to bite my tongue when my well-meaning husband haphazardly hangs clothes in the closets.

The second rule, persistence, takes more discipline.

It's much more fun to leave the tedium of unwrapping glassware for the pleasure of uncrating favorite books. But short-term enthusiasm soon turns into frustration when you still don't have a single livable room at the end of a long day.

Let me add a third rule: Stop to savor your accomplishments. As each room is completed, reward yourself and your family with a well-deserved rest break. Do something fun. It can be as uncomplicated as taking a walk around the block, enjoying an ice-cream cone, or playing Frisbee with the dog.

Above all else, remind yourself that disorganization — the second D of moving — is a temporary condition. It too shall pass.

9
Being Discouraged

"I can sum up moving in one word," a dear friend recently confided. "Discouraging!" She's right.

Even the smoothest move has its disheartening moments. At no other time in our lives does change seem ever-present and chaos never-ending. Unpacking, adjusting to a new job, and being supportive of our families can drain our limited reservoirs of optimism and good cheer.

Moving isn't an instant process. Overcoming discouragement doesn't happen quickly either. We can learn, however, to weather both and be overwhelmed by neither.

My Italian grandfather used to say that if we take care of the inches, we won't have to worry about the miles. When discouraged, we can teach ourselves to take moving in bite-sized chunks instead of trying to swallow it whole.

☐ **Don't look at the total picture.** Refuse to dwell on all that needs to be done and focus instead on one chore, one step, or one problem at a time. Breaking large jobs into smaller units lets you measure progress with a kinder yardstick.

☐ **Put this move in perspective.** Remember other times when you faced a steady stream of changes, and chaos was the only constant in your life. Reassure yourself that change turns into routine, and chaos gives way to order.

☐ **Don't worry about tomorrow.** One of the most profound lessons in the Bible takes only two sentences: "Don't be anxious about tomorrow, for tomorrow will worry about itself. Since each day has enough trouble of its own, live one day at a time." Tackle today's moving-related challenges, and leave the rest alone.

☐ **Red-flag your negative thoughts.** Whenever self-defeating thoughts enter your mind, chase them away. When you hear yourself saying, "I can't," "It's impossible," "I'm losing control," "How will I ever . . . ," bring those ideas to a screeching halt. Remind yourself that you can and will find your way through the present difficulties.

☐ **Be realistic.** Don't confuse wishful thinking with positive thinking. Wishing offers no concrete plans for reaching your goals. Positive thoughts, on the other hand, lead to workable alternatives and solutions.

☐ **Look beyond yourself.** If you're thinking, "God knows why we had to move," you're absolutely right. God knows why you moved, and he knows how to make your move successful. Don't give in to discouragement because you can't see the end from the beginning. Ask God to direct you. And if you've never done so before, now is a good time to start.

When we practice each of these small exercises, we'll discover big results. Buoyant thoughts and confident actions will slowly replace the third D of moving — Discouragement.

10

Being Disconnected

"Loneliness is the first thing which God's eye named not good," John Milton wrote three centuries ago. We probably wouldn't choose these words to describe loneliness today, but our feelings about it remain much the same.

Moving can be painfully lonely. It cuts us off from our past, isolates us in the present, and detaches us from the future. For singles and families, young and old, loneliness is the number-one problem associated with moving.

During a workshop I led for new hospice workers, I asked why they volunteered. Instead of hearing stories about loved ones dying or seeing the need for this service in their community, I heard confessions of unabashed loneliness:

"I didn't know one other person in town."

"I was tired of merely waving to the neighbors and exchanging pleasantries with sales clerks."

"Quite frankly, I needed friends as much as I needed to give of myself."

Although their comments surprised me, I applauded their honesty. I, too, could remember when the phone never rang, when I could no longer share my feelings with a trusted friend, when invitations to people's homes were scarce, when evenings and weekends stretched empty before me.

The first few weeks after a move are the most difficult. During this time, we can easily fall victim to what Joann, a hospice volunteer, labeled "The Claire Syndrome" in honor of her sister.

After moving far from friends, Claire spent her first six months isolated from everyone but her coworkers. As her loneliness deepened, so did

Claire expected immediate acceptance.

her depression. She began to dislike her new community, her job, and the few people with whom she had daily contact.

Claire never made a healthy transition to her new home. When her husband accepted a job transfer two years later, she was overjoyed. Yet her next move was no more successful.

"Claire expected immediate acceptance, friendships, and intimacy. There's no such thing where moving is concerned," Joann said. "I vowed that if my turn to move ever came, I'd not repeat her mistake. Moving hurts, and I wasn't going to make it worse!"

Joann instinctively knew that we can't help feeling disconnected in a new place, but we certainly can alter our response. Rather than feeling sorry for ourselves, we can welcome the move as a chance to expand our friendships and broaden our experiences.

When we meet the fourth D of moving — Disconnection — we don't have to give in to "The Claire Syndrome." We can choose to change our attitude, shift our focus, and reconnect.

Changing our attitude could make all the difference.

Shortly before my husband and I were to move cross-country, we met two couples who had lived in the very same county to which we were going.

The first couple, a gloomy pair, offered nothing but complaints. The weather was dreadful, the countryside blighted, and the people cold.

Then we met the second couple.

With misty eyes and wavering voices, they spoke

of the invigorating climate and lovely, rolling countryside. They recalled the warm and generous people who had become their friends and neighbors.

Our attitudes have the power to color our perceptions, thoughts and actions. In moving, we have the wonderful chance to paint our new world positive.

11

Befriending

A neighbor cross-stitched a sampler for our family shortly before we moved. As we drove across the country to our new home, the verse Nancy had stitched with such care ran through my mind:
Make new friends and keep the old.
The new are silver, the old are gold.

Nancy's thoughtfulness warmed me over the miles, but something about the sampler's words didn't. The words *make* and *keep* were the problem. How can we hope to make or keep a friend until we know how to *be* a friend?

During the remainder of the trip, I pondered what being a friend means to me.

It's willingness to laugh and cry with others.

It's sensitivity — wanting to please others with thoughtful acts and ready to leave them alone when they need solitude.

It's eagerness to praise others' talents and reluctance to criticize their shortcomings.

It's companionship that allows others to think

At no time is being a friend more important than during crises.

aloud or sit in peaceful silence.

What a lovely word *befriend* is! Volumes of wisdom are locked into that particular arrangement of eight letters. But no matter how lovely, befriending isn't automatic. It requires a lifetime of learning and growing.

To be a friend, we choose to act in three specific ways toward other people. We make the *time* to develop relationships. We take the *trouble* to give of ourselves. And we *treat* others as we would like to be treated.

Befriending means that we schedule into our busy lives the hours needed to know others better. We don't listen to friends with one eye on the clock. We don't leave their phone messages and letters unanswered because our days are too full.

Like bank accounts, friendships are built on what we invest.

At no time is being a friend more important than during life's crises. Someone once said that trouble is a big sieve through which we sift our acquaintances. Only those who are too big to pass through are friends.

When we befriend in times of trouble, we place other people's needs before our own. We support our friends as we wish to be supported. We aren't afraid to show them kindness, understanding, or care.

By giving, we receive. Being a friend, we unite with others to form a protective circle that can drive away the loneliness of moving.

12

Reconnecting

Once a week I work with a talented group of seniors in the local high school. In between conferences last week, I overheard one young man lament, "Growing friendships is a tough business."

Curious, I asked this student about his comment.

"My father owns a nursery," he replied. "I guess I'm picking up his habit. He grows plants. He grows friendships. He even grows marriage and his golf game. My father talks weird," he added with a smile.

Weird or not, I like the idea of growing friendships. It makes me realize that relationships, like plants, flourish in the proper environment.

Before we can practice being a friend, we have to discover where friendships will spring up in our new communities. Of all the challenges brought on by moving, finding friends is the most mystifying. We simply don't know where to look for those special companions of mind, heart, and spirit, people whom writer George Eliot called "wellsprings in the wilderness."

To grow friendships, we have to look inward before we can step outward. If we first take inventory of favorite hobbies, work interests, and sports, we can then seek people who share our preferences.

Potential friends are everywhere. But connecting with them will happen only when we share common interests and goals. Lectures sponsored by the city zoo, a Bible study class, a ski club, or community-service associations (such as Rotary or Chambers of Commerce) all reflect the concerns of their members. These and similar groups warmly welcome newcomers.

A good church is often one of the best places to find new friends. As members of a growing worldwide family, Christians reach out to people who are looking for practical help, for relationships, for meaning.

Joining an existing group is not the only way to reconnect.

A senior citizen whom I admire recently moved in with her son and his family. In order to meet new friends her own age, and get some exercise as well, she formed a walking club that meets at the local shopping mall.

Bonnie, the wife of an insurance executive who has been transferred often, told me about the contract she and her family developed to help them reconnect.

Each family member agrees to be involved in at least three activities within the first six months after

Seek others who share your hobbies, interests and goals.

moving. These are the varied choices they made after moving last year: Boy Scouts, a part-time job, karate lessons, Sunday school, wrestling, an evening cooking class, and membership in two professional organizations.

Growing new friendships is not really such a tough business. We must simply be willing to seek others who share our values, interests, talents, or concerns.

13
Moving Forward

In her well-organized fashion, my sister Shirley labels events in her life either *before the move* or *after the move*.

No matter how we label it, moving has a major place in our lives, dividing the passage of time into distinct "before" and "after" sections.

Before the move, we had control over our lives. After the move, we know what feeling powerless is all about.

Before the move, our lives had stability. After the move, instability is the norm.

Before the move, we were connected to people and places. After the move, we are isolated and lonely.

At some point we realize that simply facing the pain of *after the move* doesn't abolish it. That is when we begin to look beyond ourselves for the answer. We help ourselves best when we take the focus away from ourselves and place it on other people.

Before or after the move, we live in a hurting

world where people's physical, emotional and spiritual needs are rarely met. Yet we can help.

Most cultures teach a version of the Golden Rule: Do unto others as you would have them do unto you. Jesus put it this way: "Love your neighbor as yourself."

In our new communities, food banks, soup kitchens, shelters for the homeless, nursing homes, illiteracy and drug programs, and mental-health hotlines need our help. Organizations such as the Salvation Army and Red Cross need the gifts of our time and energy.

If we give our time and attention to others, we will not feel uprooted for long.

14

Flourishing Anew

There's a wonderful old church in my town. I've admired its architecture since moving here. Yet only yesterday I discovered something new about the building.

Chiseled into the stone above the massive oak doors are two messages. On the left, *Enter to Worship.* On the right, *Depart to Serve.*

Oblivious to the biting winter wind, I stood in front of the church thinking about the generations of transplanted people touched by those six simple words.

The words reminded me that moving doesn't have to be a lonely, frightening, or negative experience. In the midst of change, we can be confident in an unchanging God. He is as near as the Bible and as close as our own hearts.

No matter where we move or what we experience, we can have this one anchor of stability in the midst

Your new community will become home.

Keeping your Balance

☐ Balance means that we don't cling to the past, grumble about the present, or fear the future.

☐ Balance means that we systematically get organized, put setbacks in perspective, orient ourselves to our new environment, and reach out to others.

☐ Balance means that in searching for our basic purpose for living, we learn to care sincerely about our new town, neighbors, and workplace.

Finding this balance of trust in God and service to others, we can't help living a satisfying new life.

of a discouraging, disorienting, disorganized, and disconnected time. With God as our guide, we can struggle through the adversities of moving, welcome change, and thrive.

To do this, we need the balance that this stone message implies.

On the one hand, we need to take quiet moments for reflection, friendship, worship, and appreciating the good things we discover in our new community. This is how we fill our physical, spiritual, and mental reservoirs.

On the other hand, we need to use our energies to serve our new community and help the people around us.

Later, after pondering the message carved above the church doors, I stopped to buy groceries. As I left the supermarket, a light snow gently dusted the ground. Christmas decorations glowed in the twilight, spreading an aura of warmth and good cheer.

Smiling at this lovely scene, I received friendly nods and grins from passers-by. Suddenly I realized how familiar everything here had grown.

My new community had become home.

I shouldn't have felt surprise. Moving gives us the incredible opportunity to experience change, grow through it, and put down strong roots. Every person who moves receives this unconditional offer to flourish anew.

When such a challenge comes our way, let's meet it head-on — with honesty, creativity, hard work, and joy.